I0149951

Teacup Persian Cats

Teacup Persian Cat Breeding, Where to Buy, Types, Care, Temperament, Cost, Health, Showing, Grooming, Diet and Much More Included!

By Lolly Brown

Copyrights and Trademarks

All rights reserved. No part of this book may be reproduced or transformed in any form or by any means, graphic, electronic, or mechanical, including photocopying, recording, taping, or by any information storage retrieval system, without the written permission of the author.

This publication is Copyright ©2016 NRB Publishing, an imprint. Nevada. All products, graphics, publications, software and services mentioned and recommended in this publication are protected by trademarks. In such instance, all trademarks & copyright belong to the respective owners. For information consult www.NRBpublishing.com

Disclaimer and Legal Notice

This product is not legal, medical, or accounting advice and should not be interpreted in that manner. You need to do your own due-diligence to determine if the content of this product is right for you. While every attempt has been made to verify the information shared in this publication, neither the author, neither publisher, nor the affiliates assume any responsibility for errors, omissions or contrary interpretation of the subject matter herein. Any perceived slights to any specific person(s) or organization(s) are purely unintentional.

We have no control over the nature, content and availability of the web sites listed in this book. The inclusion of any web site links does not necessarily imply a recommendation or endorse the views expressed within them. We take no responsibility for, and will not be liable for, the websites being temporarily unavailable or being removed from the internet.

The accuracy and completeness of information provided herein and opinions stated herein are not guaranteed or warranted to produce any particular results, and the advice and strategies, contained herein may not be suitable for every individual. Neither the author nor the publisher shall be liable for any loss incurred as a consequence of the use and application, directly or indirectly, of any information presented in this work. This publication is designed to provide information in regard to the subject matter covered.

Neither the author nor the publisher assume any responsibility for any errors or omissions, nor do they represent or warrant that the ideas, information, actions, plans, suggestions contained in this book is in all cases accurate. It is the reader's responsibility to find advice before putting anything written in this book into practice. The information in this book is not intended to serve as legal, medical, or accounting advice.

Foreword

The Persian cat breed is one of the most popular cat breeds out there, loved for its plush coat and large eyes. These cats are a calm, quiet breed that adapts well to apartment life and are generally friendly toward strangers and affectionate with their owners. If you are looking for a friendly, loving cat breed that will stop at nothing to become your very best friend, the Teacup Persian just might be the perfect choice.

If you think that the Teacup Persian might be the right breed for you, take the time to learn as much about these wonderful pets as you can. In this book you will find a wealth of information about this unique and beautiful cat breed including general facts about the breed, its history, and practical information for keeping Teacup Persian cats. By the time you finish this book you will have a thorough understanding of the Teacup Persian breed and you will know for sure whether or not the Sphynx cat is for you.

So, if you are ready to learn more about the Teacup Persian cat breed, turn the page and keep reading!

Table of Contents

Introduction

When you picture the Persian cat breed do you imagine a large cat with a long, plush coat of luxurious white fur? Or do you picture a ginger-coated cat with a set of bright blue eyes? Both of these descriptions are fitting for the Persian cat breed but they are just a few of the many colors and patterns these cats are known for. Not only do Persian cats come in all kinds of colors and patterns, but they also come in different sizes. The Teacup Persian is a miniaturized version of the Persian cat breed and it is rapidly gaining in popularity.

The Teacup Persian may not be recognized as a unique breed by the Cat Fanciers' Association (CFA), but they are different from traditional Persians in a number of ways. Not only are Teacup Persians much smaller than the traditional Persian cat, but they are particularly well adapted to apartment and condo life. Though they may be small, Teacup Persians have big, friendly personalities just like their larger cousins. They also come in every color and pattern you can possibly imagine.

If you think that the Teacup Persian might be the right breed for you, take the time to learn as much about these wonderful pets as you can. In this book you will find a wealth of information about this unique and beautiful cat breed including general facts about the breed, its history, and practical information for keeping Teacup Persian cats. By the time you finish this book you will have a thorough understanding of the Teacup Persian breed and you will know for sure whether or not the Teacup Persian cat is for you.

So, if you are ready to learn more about the Teacup Persian cat breed simply turn the page and keep reading!

Glossary of Cat Terms

Abundism – Referring to a cat that has markings more prolific than is normal.

Acariasis – A type of mite infection.

ACF – Australian Cat Federation

Affix – A cattery name that follows the cat's registered name; cattery owner, not the breeder of the cat.

Agouti – A type of natural coloring pattern in which individual hairs have bands of light and dark coloring.

Ailurophile – A person who loves cats.

Albino – A type of genetic mutation which results in little to no pigmentation, in the eyes, skin, and coat.

Allbreed – Referring to a show that accepts all breeds or a judge who is qualified to judge all breeds.

Alley Cat – A non-pedigreed cat.

Alter – A desexed cat; a male cat that has been neutered or a female that has been spayed.

Amino Acid – The building blocks of protein; there are 22 types for cats, 11 of which can be synthesized and 11 which must come from the diet (see essential amino acid).

Anestrus – The period between estrus cycles in a female cat.

Any Other Variety (AOV) – A registered cat that doesn't conform to the breed standard.

ASH – American Shorthair, a breed of cat.

Back Cross – A type of breeding in which the offspring is mated back to the parent.

Balance – Referring to the cat's structure; proportional in accordance with the breed standard.

Barring – Describing the tabby's striped markings.

Base Color – The color of the coat.

Bicolor – A cat with patched color and white.

Blaze – A white coloring on the face, usually in the shape of an inverted V.

Bloodline – The pedigree of the cat.

Brindle – A type of coloring, a brownish or tawny coat with streaks of another color.

Castration – The surgical removal of a male cat's testicles.

Cat Show – An event where cats are shown and judged.

Cattery – A registered cat breeder; also, a place where cats may be boarded.

CFA – The Cat Fanciers Association.

Cobby – A compact body type.

Colony – A group of cats living wild outside.

Color Point – A type of coat pattern that is controlled by color point alleles; pigmentation on the tail, legs, face, and ears with an ivory or white coat.

Colostrum – The first milk produced by a lactating female; contains vital nutrients and antibodies.

Conformation – The degree to which a pedigreed cat adheres to the breed standard.

Cross Breed – The offspring produced by mating two distinct breeds.

Dam – The female parent.

Declawing – The surgical removal of the cat's claw and first toe joint.

Developed Breed – A breed that was developed through selective breeding and crossing with established breeds.

Down Hairs – The short, fine hairs closest to the body which keep the cat warm.

DSH – Domestic Shorthair.

Estrus – The reproductive cycle in female cats during which she becomes fertile and receptive to mating.

Fading Kitten Syndrome – Kittens that die within the first two weeks after birth; the cause is generally unknown.

Feral – A wild, untamed cat of domestic descent.

Gestation – Pregnancy; the period during which the fetuses develop in the female's uterus.

Guard Hairs – Coarse, outer hairs on the coat.

Harlequin – A type of coloring in which there are van markings of any color with the addition of small patches of the same color on the legs and body.

Inbreeding – The breeding of related cats within a closed group or breed.

Kibble – Another name for dry cat food.

Lilac – A type of coat color that is pale pinkish-gray.

Line – The pedigree of ancestors; family tree.

Litter – The name given to a group of kittens born at the same time from a single female.

Mask – A type of coloring seen on the face in some breeds.

Matts – Knots or tangles in the cat's fur.

Mittens – White markings on the feet of a cat.

Moggie – Another name for a mixed breed cat.

Mutation – A change in the DNA of a cell.

Mutation Breed – A breed of cat that resulted from a spontaneous mutation; ex: Cornish Rex and Sphynx.

Muzzle – The nose and jaws of an animal.

Natural Breed – A breed that developed without selective breeding or the assistance of humans.

Neutering – Desexing a male cat.

Open Show – A show in which spectators are allowed to view the judging.

Pads – The thick skin on the bottom of the feet.

Particolor – A type of coloration in which there are markings of two or more distinct colors.

Patched – A type of coloration in which there is any solid color, tabby, or tortoiseshell color plus white.

Pedigree – A purebred cat; the cat's papers showing its family history.

Pet Quality – A cat that is not deemed of high enough standard to be shown or bred.

Piebald – A cat with white patches of fur.

Points – Also color points; markings of contrasting color on the face, ears, legs, and tail.

Pricked – Referring to ears that sit upright.

Purebred – A pedigreed cat.

Queen – An intact female cat.

Roman Nose – A type of nose shape with a bump or arch.

Scruff – The loose skin on the back of a cat's neck.

Selective Breeding – A method of modifying or improving a breed by choosing cats with desirable traits.

Senior – A cat that is more than 5 but less than 7 years old.

Sire – The male parent of a cat.

Solid – Also self; a cat with a single coat color.

Spay – Desexing a female cat.

Stud – An intact male cat.

Tabby – A type of coat pattern consisting of a contrasting color over a ground color.

Tom Cat – An intact male cat.

Tortoiseshell – A type of coat pattern consisting of a mosaic of red or cream and another base color.

Tri-Color – A type of coat pattern consisting of three distinct colors in the coat.

Tuxedo – A black and white cat.

Unaltered – A cat that has not been desexed.

Chapter One: Teacup Persian Basics

Few breeds are as beautiful as the Persian cat with its long, luxurious coat but this breed is not the right choice for everyone. Before you decide to get a Persian cat for yourself of your family, you need to learn everything you can about these wonderful creatures. In this chapter you will receive an overview of the Persian cat breed with details about its appearance, personality and temperament. You will also find a history of the breed and a breakdown of Persian variants, related breeds, and hybrid breeds.

Facts About Teacup Persian Cats

Not only is the Persian cat one of the most beautiful cats in the world, but it is also one of the most popular breeds. This breed is known as much for its long, flowing coat as its sweet, friendly personality. These cats are gentle and quiet by nature which makes them a great family pet, plus they are very people-oriented and they love to cuddle. Persian cats are the ideal lap cat, though they do have a bit of a goofy side if you take the time to play with them. These cats generally don't jump or climb, so you don't have to worry too much out them destroying your furniture.

If you want to get into the nitty gritty details, there are actually two types of Persian cat – the kind used for show and the traditional pet type. Show Persians have large, round heads with a thick ruff and a broad, short body. They have small ears, flattened noses, and large round copper-colored eyes. It is all finished off with a thick plume tail. The traditional Persian, sometimes known as the doll-face type, has less extreme features and a normal-length muzzle that gives him a decidedly sweet expression. Both the show and traditional types have long, luscious coats and they come in a variety of colors and patterns.

Not only is the Persian cat available in a show type or a traditional type, but there is also a smaller version of the breed known as the Teacup Persian. Persian cats are usually medium-sized, growing to a maximum size around 7 to 12 pounds. Teacup Persians, on the other hand, only grow to weigh about 3 to 5 pounds on average for a female, and up to 8 pound for a male. They get their name from the fact that they are small enough to fit into a teacup when they are kittens, but they will outgrow the teacup by the time they reach maturity around 1 year of age.

Though they may differ from traditional Persians in terms of their size, Teacup Persians are largely identical in every other way. These cats have fairly short, broad bodies with short legs and a plumed tail. Their coats grow long so they need to be brushed on a daily basis to prevent tangling and mats – you may also need to bathe your cat several times a month to keep his coat in good condition. If you don't want to tackle this task yourself, you can take your cat to a professional groomer.

When it comes to typical coat colors and patterns, Persians and Teacup Persians exhibit all colors of the rainbow. These cats may have solid-color coats in various shades of white, brown, gray, or black but they may also have a colorpoint pattern similar to the Siamese cat (this is usually called Himalayan coloration). Persian cats can exhibit a tabby pattern or a calico pattern, and they may be bi-colored in a variety of different shades. Teacup Persians can also come in all of the same colors and patterns as their larger Persian relatives.

In terms of personality, Teacup Persians are incredibly gentle and affectionate with their families. They get along with pretty much everyone they meet, including dogs and children, and they are wonderful lap cats. Due to their size and laidback nature, these cats adapt well to urban or condo life and they generally do well when left alone for hours at a time, though the definitely prefer to be in the company of humans. If you have to leave town, it is generally better to leave a Persian cat with a pet sitter than to board him in a kennel.

Persian cats in general are prone to a number of serious health problems and some of them are worse in Teacup Persians due to their smaller size. In terms of hereditary health issues, the most common problems seen in the Persian and Teacup Persian breed include polycystic kidney disease (PKD), hypertrophic cardiomyopathy, progressive retinal atrophy, and liver shunts. These cats may also develop cystitis (or bladder infections), bladder stones, and various eye conditions. Due to their thick coats, these cats are also sensitive to heat so they need to be kept in air conditioning during the summer.

Summary of Teacup Persian Cat Facts

Pedigree: same breed as the Persian cat but selectively bred down in size for Teacup variety

Breed Size: small

Weight: 3 to 5 pounds for females, up to 8 pounds for males

Coat Length: long

Coat Texture: very soft, silky and luxurious

Color: comes in a wide variety of solid and bi-color patterns including Himalayan, tabby, tortoiseshell, and more

Eyes and Nose: eyes are large and round, color is usually copper or blue; nose color varies by coloration

Ears: small with rounded tips

Tail: long and plumed

Temperament: gentle, quiet, laidback, lazy, affectionate, people-oriented, loving

Strangers: typically warms up quickly

Children: generally patient as long as the child knows how to properly handle a cat; may not tolerate rough handling

Other Pets: can do well when raised together

Exercise Needs: fairly low

Health Conditions: polycystic kidney disease (PKD), hypertrophic cardiomyopathy, progressive retinal atrophy, liver shunts, cystitis, bladder stones, eye conditions, dental malocclusions, seborrhea oleosa

Lifespan: 10 to 15 years average

Teacup Persian Cat Breed History

The Persian cat is a longhaired breed and the exact origins of longhaired cats are unknown. The first documented examples of a Persian-type cat were imported into Italy from Khorasan, Persia (now known as Iran) as far back as 1620. At the same time, ancestors of the breed were imported from Angora, Turkey (now known as Ankara) into France. Most of the cats from Khorasan had grey coats while those form Angora were largely white. These two varieties eventually came to be known as different breeds – the Persian and the Angora cat.

The very first Persian cat appeared at the first cat show held in 1871 at the Crystal Palace in London. In the years that followed, efforts were made to distinguish the Persian type from the Angora type and the first official breed standard was issued in 1889, developed by cat show promoter Harrison Weir. In this breed standard it was made clear that Persian cats had longer tails, fuller and coarser coats, larger heads, and more rounded ears. Even with the breed standard, however, many cat fanciers didn't immediately accept the differentiation between the two types and some breeders chose to interpret the Persian type in different ways.

In Italy, Germany, and the United States, the so-called traditional Persian cat had a flat-nosed look sometimes known as "peke-face" (also known as the "ultra" type) which was the result of several genetic mutations. This characteristic appeared during the late 1950s as a spontaneous mutation in red and red tabby Persian cats and it was named after the flat-faced look of the Pekingese dog breed. Originally, the peke-faced Persian was registered as a separate breed with the Cat Fanciers' Association (CFA) but it declined in popularity due to serious health problems until, by the mid-1990s, there were fewer than 100 Persian cats registered.

Although different types for the breed have come and gone over the years, the Persian Breed Council's standard for the breed has remained largely unchanged. The Persian breed standard is somewhat open-ended, though it does pinpoint a few key features such as a rounded head, large widely-spaced eyes, a short cobby body, and a broad chest. It wasn't until the early 2000s that rules about the flat-faced type were added to the breed standard. Today, ultra-type Persians tend to do best in shows, though the public tends to prefer the less extreme doll-face type as a pet.

Persian Cat Variants and Related Breeds

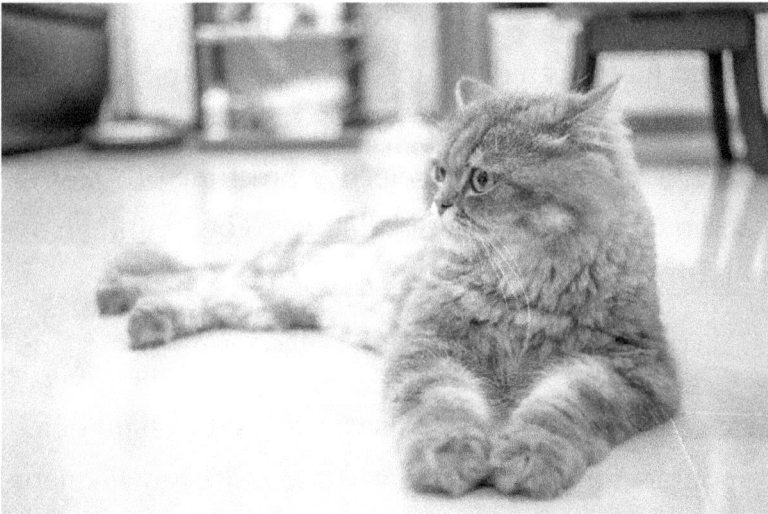

You don't have to be a dog owner to know that there are a variety of distinct dog breeds out there. But many people do not realize that there are a number of distinct cat breeds as well. In many cases, the differences between various breeds of cat are more nuanced than the differences between dog breeds, but they exist nonetheless. What can sometimes be tricky is the fact that several different cat breeds are considered variants of a single breed – this is the case for the Persian cat.

a.) Variants of the Persian Breed

The origins of the Persian breed can be traced back to the early 1620s so it is no wonder that several variants of the breed have been developed over the years. All of these variants are descended from the same ancestors, but various genetic mutations and selective breeding processes yielded some very unique results. Below you will find an overview of different variants of the Persian breed:

Peke-Faced Persian – This variant is the result of a spontaneous mutation in red and red tabby Persians that developed during the 1950s. Peke-faced Persians have a flat face with virtually no muzzle – they also have wrinkles above the nose and bulging eyes. While once popular, few breeders are currently developing this breed because they are prone to a number of serious health problems and the peke-faced look is no longer fashionable.

Persian Longhair – This type was known as the Asiatic cat (or Turkish Angora) until the 1870s and it is the type of Persian cat that was introduced into Europe from Asian Minor. During the early 1900s, breeders began to differentiate the breed from the Turkish Angora type, giving it a larger, more cobby body type. The breed is known as the Persian Longhair in the U.K. simply to differentiate it from other long-haired breeds.

Persian Ticked – This type of Persian has ticked markings in a range of colors which is accomplished by crossing the Persian Longhair with the Somali cat breed. This pattern is very different from the typical tipped, shaded, and smoke patterns usually seen in Persian Longhairs.

Teacup Persian – This is the name given to Persian cats that have been selectively bred for their small size. These cats are also known as "pocket", "palm-sized", and "pixie" cats and they are generally not considered a distinct breed.

b.) Persian Hybrid Breeds

Not only are there a number of different variants of the Persian cat breed out there, but there are also a number of hybrid breeds. A hybrid breed is created by crossing two purebred cats of different breeds. Technically, you can create a hybrid of the Persian breed by crossing it with any other breed but there are a limited number of combination that have become popular enough to warrant their own name. Below you will find a brief overview of the top six hybrid breeds developed from the Persian type:

Himalayan – This breed is the result of crossing a Persian cat with a Siamese and it was developed in the 1950s. Essentially, the Himalayan cat has the body type of the Persian but the color points of a Siamese cat. In the United Kingdom, this breed is recognized as the Colorpoint Longhair, not as a separate breed. In the United States, it was a separate breed until 1984 when the CFA merged it with the Persian breed for registration.

Exotic Shorthair – This hybrid was created in the 1950s by crossing the Persian with the American Shorthair (ASH) as a means of improving the ASH breed. This breed is similar to the Persian in every way including conformation and temperament but it differs in terms of its short, dense coat which is much easier to manage than the Persian's long coat.

Due to genetics, however, there is a 1-in-4 chance that Exotic Shorthair kittens will be born with a long coat.

Napoleon – The Napoleon cat breed is named for its short stature which it gets from a crossing of the Persian breed and the Munchkin breed. This breed is also known as the Minuet cat and it has a doll-like face, a low-slung body, and a sweet personality. These cats are very gentle and affectionate as well as being incredibly people-oriented – they make great family pets.

Ragdoll – This breed is the result of a cross between the Persian and Birman cat breeds and it is one of the largest breeds of cat. Ragdoll cats are semi-longhaired and they have beautiful blue eyes. This breed is extremely friendly, getting along with dogs as well as children, and they are very adaptable for busy families. Ragdoll cats are quiet and loving with a very laidback disposition.

Alaskan Snow Cat – This is a cross between the Somali cat and the silver Persian cat and it was created in the 1990s in the United States. The Alaskan Snow Cat typically has a white underbelly, though the rest of its coloration varies from rusty brown to black, and there are usually dark bands on the legs and tail. The most desirable color for this breed is silver-gray with dark gray bands and a pure white belly.

Per-Manx – This breed is a cross between the Persian cat and the Manx breed – it generally results in a tailless Persian-type cat. There have also been cases of spontaneous mutation where Persian kittens are born without tails.

Teacup Persian Colors

While some cat breeds come in a single color (like the beautiful black Bombay), the Persian and Teacup Persian comes in a wide range of different colors. Below you will find a brief description of some of the most popular solid colorations taken from the CFA standard for the breed:

- **White (Solid)** – Pure white with pink nose leather and paw pads. Eyes are deep blue or copper.
- **Blue (Solid)** – Lighter shades preferred, sound to the roots. Nose leather and paw pads are blue, eyes copper.
- **Black (Solid)** – Dense coal black, sound to the roots. Nose leather is black, paw pads are brown or black, eyes copper.
- **Red (Solid)** – Deep and clear red without shading or makings. Nose leather and paw pads are brick red, eyes copper.
- **Cream (Solid)** – One level shade of cream buff, no markings, lighter shades preferred. Nose leather and paw pads are pink, eyes copper.
- **Chocolate (Solid)** – Rich chocolate-brown, sound to the roots. Nose leather is brown, paw pads cinnamon-pink, eyes copper.
- **Lilac (Solid)** -Warm lavender, sound throughout. Nose leather is lavender, paw pads pink, eyes copper.

In addition to the solid colors described on the previous page, the Persian cat also comes in a number of patterned colorations. Here is a quick list of some of the other colorations seen in this breed:

- **Silver and Gold Division** – chinchilla silver, shaded silver, blue chinchilla silver, blue shaded silver, chinchilla golden, shaded golden, blue chinchilla golden, blue shaded golden
- **Shaded and Smoke Division** – shell cameo, shaded cameo, shell cream, shaded cream, shell tortoiseshell, shaded tortoiseshell, shell blue-cream, shaded blue-cream, black smoke, blue smoke, red smoke, tortoiseshell smoke, blue-cream smoke, chocolate smoke, lilac smoke, chocolate tortoiseshell smoke, lilac-cream smoke
- **Tabby Division** – classic tabby, mackerel tabby, silver tabby, silver patched tabby, blue-silver tabby, blue-silver patched tabby, red tabby, brown tabby, brown patched tabby, blue tabby, blue patched tabby, cream tabby, cameo tabby, cream silver tabby, chocolate tabby, chocolate patched tabby, lilac tabby, lilac patched tabby
- **Parti-Color Division** – tortoiseshell, blue-cream, chocolate tortoiseshell, lilac-cream
- **Calico and Bi-Color Division** – calico, dilute calico, chocolate calico, lilac calico, bi-color, smoke and white, calico smoke, dilute calico smoke, chocolate calico smoke, lilac calico smoke, shell cameo, shaded cameo, red tabby and white, brown tabby and white, patched tabby and white, other tabby and white

- **Himalayan Division** – Himalayan pattern, chocolate point, seal point, lilac point, blue point, flame point, cream point, tortie point, blue-cream point, chocolate-tortie point, lilac-cream point, Himalayan lynx point, seal lynx point, blue lynx point, flame lynx point, cream lynx point, tortie lynx point, blue-cream lynx point, chocolate lynx point, lilac lynx point, chocolate-tortie lynx point, lilac-cream lynx point

Chapter Two: Things to Know Before Getting a Teacup Persian Cat

Having a basic understanding of the Teacup Persian and its background, you may be thinking that it is the right breed for you. Before you actually make your decision, however, you need to consider the practical aspects of owning a Persian cat. Do they get along with other pets? How much do they cost? And what are the pros and cons for the breed? You will learn these things and more in this chapter which will help you to make an educated decision about whether this is the best breed for you.

Do You Need a License?

Before you bring home a new pet, you always need to make sure that it is legal for you to keep it in your area. Licensing requirements for pets are different in different countries, regions, and states so do not assume you know the rules. In the United States there are no federal requirements for licensing either cats or dogs – these rules are regulated at the state level. While it is true that most states do not have a mandatory requirement for people to license their cats, it is always a good idea to do so.

When you license your cat you will be giving your cat a number that can then be linked to your contact information. If your cat gets lost and someone finds him, his license can be used to track you down and to reunite you with your pet. Of course, this information will only be available if your cat wears a collar with an ID tag. If you don't want to put a collar on your cat a good alternative is to have him microchipped. A microchip serves the same function but they can be embedded under your cat's skin so he can't lose it. The procedure for having your cat microchipped is very quick and painless.

In the United Kingdom, licensing requirements for pets are a little different than they are in the United States. There are no overarching licensing requirements for cats in the U.K. but you will need to get a special permit if you plan to travel with your cat into or out of the country. Your cat may also be subject to a quarantine period to make sure he isn't carrying a disease like rabies – rabies has been eradicated from the U.K. through safety measures like these so it is important to maintain them.

How Many Teacup Persian Cats Should You Keep?

This is a common question that cat owners ask when they are forced to spend a lot of time away from home. Teacup Persians are not a high-energy breed so they don't need a lot of daily exercise, but they are a very people-oriented breed so they may suffer if left alone for long periods of time on a regular basis. Teacup Persian cats generally get along with other cats since they are so passive and gentle-mannered, but getting a second cat to keep your Teacup Persian company may not always be the best idea. You'll need to take your individual cat's personality into consideration.

Do Teacup Persian Cats Get Along with Other Pets?

In most cases, Teacup Persians will not cause problems with other pets if they are left alone themselves. Teacup Persians do have the capacity to get along with mild-mannered dogs and they can tolerate other cats as well. When it comes to small household pets like rodents and birds, however, you may want to exercise some caution. Even if your Teacup Persian doesn't seem to show much interest in these pets, you should always supervise interactions to be safe.

How Much Does It Cost to Keep a Teacup Persian Cat?

If you have never owned a cat before, you may be tempted to think that it is a minor expense. If you tally up the costs of purchasing a well-bred kitten, stocking up on food and toys, providing a cat bed, and taking your cat to the vet twice a year, the costs add up quickly! Before you bring home a Teacup Persian cat you should be sure that you can provide for his needs financially. In this section you will receive an overview of the initial costs and monthly costs for keeping a cat so you can determine whether you are able to provide for such a cat or not.

Initial Costs

The initial costs for keeping Teacup Persian cats include the costs you have to cover before you actually bring your cat home. Some of the initial costs you will need to cover include your cat's bed, food/water bowls, toys and accessories, microchipping, initial vaccinations, spay/neuter surgery and supplies for grooming and nail clipping – it also includes the cost of the cat itself.

<u>You will find an overview of each of these costs as well as an estimate for each below</u>:

Purchase Price – The cost to purchase a cat can vary greatly depending where you buy him. You can adopt a rescue cat for as little as $50 (£45) sometimes but purchasing a kitten, especially a purebred kitten from a responsible breeder, could be much costlier. The cost of a show-quality Persian cat or one with a unique color could be as much as $1,200 (£1,080) or more while pet-quality kittens good breeding, might cost closer to $700 (£630).

If you have your heart set on a Teacup Persian, the costs could be completely different. It is important to remember that Teacup Persians are not a separate breed – they are just bred down in size. Due to the potential for health problems, responsible breeding is a must so don't plan to spend less than $500 (£450) for a Teacup Persian kitten. On the other hand, do not spend more than $800 (£720) for a pet-quality kitten.

Bed – Because the Teacup Persian is a small-sized cat you will not need a very large bed. The average cost for a small cat bed is about $30 (£19.50) in most cases.

Food/Water Bowls – In addition to providing your Teacup Persian cat with a bed to sleep in, you should also make sure he has a set of high-quality food and water bowls. The best materials for these is stainless steel because it is easy to clean and doesn't harbor bacteria – ceramic is another good option. The average cost for a quality set of stainless steel bowls is about $20 (£18).

Toys – Giving your new cat plenty of toys to play with will help to keep him from getting into trouble when he is home alone – they can also be used to provide mental stimulation and enrichment. To start out, plan to buy an assortment of toys for your cat until you learn what kind he prefers. You may want to budget a cost of $50 (£45) for toys just to be sure you have enough.

Microchipping – In the United States and United Kingdom there are no federal or state requirements saying that you have to have your cat microchipped, but it is a very good idea. Your Teacup Persian could slip outside through an open door or window without you noticing. If someone finds him without identification, they can take him to a shelter to have his microchip scanned. A microchip is something that is implanted under your cat's skin and it carries a number that is linked to your contact information. The procedure takes just a few minutes to perform and it only costs about $30 (£19.50) in most cases.

Initial Vaccinations – During your kitten's first year of life, he will require a number of different vaccinations. If you purchase your kitten from a reputable breeder, he might already have had a few but you'll still need more over the next few months as well as booster shots each year. You should budget about $50 (£32.50) for initial vaccinations just to be prepared.

Spay/Neuter Surgery – If you don't plan to breed your Teacup Persian cat you should have him or her neutered or spayed before 6 months of age. The cost for this surgery will vary depending where you go and on the sex of your cat. If you go to a traditional veterinary surgeon, the cost for spay/neuter surgery could be very high but you can save money by going to a veterinary clinic. The average cost for neuter surgery is $50 to $100 (£32.50 - £65) and spay surgery costs about $100 to $200 (£65 - £130).

Supplies/Accessories – In addition to purchasing your cat's bed and food/water bowls, you should also purchase some basic grooming supplies like nail clippers and mild, pet-safe shampoo. You might also want a collar with an ID tag. The cost for these items will vary depending on the quality, but you should budget about $100 (£32.50) for these extra costs.

Initial Costs for Teacup Persian Cats		
Cost	**One Cat**	**Two Cats**
Purchase Price	$50 - $1,200 (£45 - £1,080)	$100 - $2,400 (£90 - £2,160)
Cat Bed	$30 (£19.50)	$60 (£39)
Food/Water Bowl	$20 (£18)	$40 (£36)
Toys	$50 (£45)	$100 (£90)
Microchipping	$30 (£19.50)	$60 (£39)
Vaccinations	$50 (£32.50)	$100 (£65)
Spay/Neuter	$50 to $200 (£32.50 - £130)	$100 to $400 (£65 - £260)

Accessories	$100 (£90)	$100 (£90)
Total	$380 to $1,680 (£342 – £1,512)	$660 to $3,260 (£594 – £2,934)

*Costs may vary depending on location

**U.K. prices based on an estimated exchange of $1 = £0.90

Monthly Costs

The monthly costs for keeping a Teacup Persian cat as a pet include those costs which recur on a monthly basis. The most important monthly cost for keeping a cat is, of course, food. In addition to food, however, you'll also need to think about things like your annual license renewal, toy replacements, and veterinary exams. <u>You will find an overview of each of these costs as well as an estimate for each cost below</u>:

Food and Treats – Feeding your Teacup Persian cat a healthy diet is very important for his health and wellness. A high-quality diet for cats is not cheap, though this breed is fairly small and won't eat a lot at one time. Still, you should be prepared to spend around $35 (£31.50) on a large bag of high-quality cat food which will last you about a month. You should also include a monthly budget of about $10 (£6.50) for treats.

License Renewal – The cost to license your Teacup Persian cat will generally be about $25 (£16.25) and you can renew the license for the same price each year. License renewal cost divided over 12 months is about $2 (£1.30) per month.

Veterinary Exams – In order to keep your cat healthy you should take him to the veterinarian about every six months after he passes kittenhood. You might have to take him more often for the first 12 months to make sure he gets his vaccines on time. The average cost for a vet visit is about $40 (£26) so, if you have two visits per year, it averages to about $7 (£4.55) per month.

Other Costs – In addition to the monthly costs for your cat's food, license renewal, and vet visits there are also some other cost you might have to pay occasionally. These costs might include things like replacements for worn-out toys and cleaning products. You should budget about $15 (£9.75) per month for extra costs.

Monthly Costs for Teacup Persian Cats		
Cost	**One Cat**	**Two Cats**
Food and Treats	$45 (£40.50)	$90 (£81)

License Renewal	$2 (£1.30)	$4 (£3.60)
Veterinary Exams	$7 (£4.55)	$14 (£12.60)
Other Costs	$15 (£9.75)	$30 (£19.50)
Total	$99 (£89)	$198 (£178)

*Costs may vary depending on location
**U.K. prices based on an estimated exchange of $1 = £0.90

What are the Pros and Cons of Teacup Persian Cats?

The Teacup Persian is a beautiful breed that makes a wonderful pet, but it is not the right choice for everyone. Before you make your decision, consider the pros and cons of this breed. Below you will find an overview of the pros and cons for the Teacup Persian breed:

Pros for the Teacup Persian Cat Breed

- Small in size compared to many cats (average 3 to 8 pounds) which means they need less space (good for apartment and condo life)
- Generally, not an active or energetic breed, content to sleep the day away on the couch
- Very friendly and affectionate with family, they are a people-oriented breed
- Long, luxurious coat comes in a variety of different colors and patterns
- Usually a very quiet breeds, uses its eyes to communicate instead of meowing a lot
- Typically gets along well with gentle dogs, children, and other cats
- Can be left alone during the day but would prefer to spend time with family

Cons for the Teacup Persian Cat Breed

- Long, thick, double coat requires daily brushing and frequent bathing and grooming
- Not the most active breed if you are looking for a cat that will always be interested in playing with you
- Thick coat makes them extra sensitive to heat, not recommended as an outdoor cat

- Prone to a number of inherited health conditions, careful breeding is required
- Can sometimes be aloof around strangers but usually warms up fairly quickly
- Shedding will always be a problem with this breed

Chapter Three: Purchasing Your Teacup Persian Cat

By now you should have a clear understanding of the Persian breed and the Teacup Persian breed. Keeping this information in mind, if you think that it is the right breed for you, your next step is to decide where you are going to get your new cat. In this chapter you will receive some basic tips for finding a Teacup Persian cat breeder and for choosing one that is reputable and trustworthy. You will also receive tips for picking out a kitten that is healthy and well-bred. Finally, you will receive tips for kitten-proofing your home to get ready for your cat.

Where Can You Buy Teacup Persian Cats?

If you have decided that the Teacup Persian cat is the right breed for you and your family, you need to start thinking about where you are going to get one. The Teacup Persian cat breed is not exactly rare, but it is not common either so you should be prepared to look around a bit before you find one. When looking for a breeder that specializes in the Teacup Persian size, be very careful to see the breeding stock to make sure that they are indeed smaller Persians – you won't be able to tell by looking at the kittens whether or not they are of the teacup size.

If you are having trouble finding a breeder, you may be tempted to buy a kitten from your local pet store instead.

Be careful about purchasing kittens from pet stores because you do not know where they came from – they could come from a quality breeder but it is more likely they came from a hobby breeder or an unlicensed breeding facility that puts profits over the welfare of the animals.

In the United States, you can perform an online search for Persian cat breeders or you can check the Cat Fanciers' Association (CFA) website for an index of breeders. In the United Kingdom and in other parts of Europe, The International Cat Association (TICA) provides a list of breeders for each of its registered cat breeds. You can also try the Persian Breed Council which provides a list of breeders as well.

If you don't particularly care about bringing home a kitten, or if you want to do your part in reducing the unwanted pet population, you might want to think about adopting a cat. There are many benefits for adopting cats besides the fact that you could literally be saving a life by taking a rescue cat into your home. Many rescue cats have already been litter trained and they are often past the kitten phase as well which means that you may not have to deal with typical kitten behaviors like scratching. Rescue cats that are adults are also fully grown and developed so you can get a good feel for their personality – kittens can change in terms of their personality as they mature so you never really know what you might end up with.

If you are thinking about adopting a Teacup Persian cat, consider one of these breed-specific rescues:

United States Rescues:

Specialty Purebred Cat Rescue.
<http://www.purebredcatrescue.org/persians>

Persian and Himalayan Cat Rescue.
<http://www.persiancats.org/>

Helping Persian Cats. <http://helpingpersiancats.org/>

DFW Purebred Rescue. <http://dfwpurebredrescue.org/>

United Kingdom Rescues:

Chapelhouse Persian Rescue.
<http://www.chapelhouse-persians.co.uk/>

Rushden Persian Rescue.
<http://rushdenpersianrescue.co.uk/>

London Persian Rescue.
<http://www.london-persian-rescue.co.uk/>

Persian Rescue – Bristol.

<http://www.persianrescue.co.uk/>

St. Francis Persian Cat Rescue.

<http://www.stfrancisrescue.co.uk/>

How to Choose a Reputable Teacup Persian Cat Breeder

Though the Teacup Persian is a beautiful and gentle breed, it is a breed prone to numerous hereditary health problems. This being the case, you need to make sure to get your kitten from a reputable breeder. A reputable breeder will DNA-test his breeding stock to prevent passing these diseases on – he will also take other steps to ensure that his kittens are healthy and well-bred. In order to find a good Teacup Persian breeder, however, you may have to do a little bit of footwork.

Start by asking your local vet clinic or fellow cat owners for recommendations – if that doesn't work, a simple internet search should yield some results that you can go through. Once you've compiled a list of several breeders you then need to go through them to choose the best option. You don't want to run the risk of purchasing a kitten from a hobby breeder or from someone who doesn't follow responsible breeding practices. If you aren't careful about where you get your kitten you could end up with a kitten that is already sick. Once you have your list of breeders on hand you can go through them one-by-one to narrow down your options.

Go through the following steps to weed out low-quality breeders and to choose the best option:

- Visit the website for each breeder on your list (if they have one) and look for key information about the breeder's history and experience.
  - o Check for club registrations and a license, if applicable.
  - o If the website doesn't provide any information about the facilities or the breeder you are best just moving on.

- After ruling out some of the breeders, contact the remaining breeders on your list by phone
  - Ask the breeder questions about his experience with breeding dogs in general and about the Teacup Persian cat breed in particular.
  - Ask for information about the breeding stock including registration numbers and health information.
  - Expect a reputable breeder to ask you questions about yourself as well – a responsible breeder wants to make sure that his kittens go to good homes.
- Schedule an appointment to visit the facilities for the remaining breeders on your list after you've weeded a few more of them out.
  - Ask for a tour of the facilities, including the place where the breeding stock is kept as well as the facilities housing the kittens.
  - If things look unorganized or unclean, do not purchase from the breeder.
  - Make sure the breeding stock is in good condition and that the kittens are all healthy-looking and active.
- Narrow down your list to a final few options and then interact with the kittens to make your decision.

- o Make sure the breeder provides some kind of
     health guarantee and ask about any
     vaccinations the kittens may already have.

Once you've chosen your kitten, ask the breeder if the kittens are ready to be separated from their mother. Put down a deposit, if needed, to reserve a kitten if they aren't ready to come home yet.

Tips for Selecting a Healthy Teacup Persian Kitten

Even after you've chosen a reputable Teacup Persian breeder, your work is not done! Now you need to take the time to pick out a healthy kitten. If you don't take the time to make sure that the kitten you bring home is in good health, you could be setting yourself up for a decade of frequent vet visits and that can become very costly. Picking out a healthy kitten is not difficult and it is absolutely worth it.

Follow the steps below to pick out your Teacup Persian kitten:

- Ask the breeder to give you a tour of the facilities, especially where the kittens are kept.
  - o Make sure the facilities where the kittens are housed is clean and sanitary – if there is evidence of diarrhea, do not purchase one of the kittens because they may already be sick.
- Take a few minutes to observe the litter as a whole, watching how the kittens interact with each other.
  - o The kittens should be active and playful, interacting with each other in a healthy way.
  - o Avoid kittens that appear to be lethargic and those that have difficulty moving – they could be sick.
- Approach the litter and watch how the kittens react to you when you do.
  - o If the kittens appear frightened they may not be properly socialized and you do not want a kitten like that.
  - o The kittens may be somewhat cautious, but they should be curious and interested in you.

- Let the kittens approach you and give them time to sniff and explore you before you interact with them.
  - Pet the kittens and encourage them to play with a toy, taking the opportunity to observe their personalities.
  - Single out any of the kittens that you think might be a good fit and spend a little time with them.
- Pick up the kitten and hold him to see how he responds to human contact.
  - The kitten might squirm a little but it shouldn't be frightened of you and it should enjoy being pet.
- Examine the kitten's body for signs of any illness and potential injury
  - The kitten should have clear, bright eyes with no discharge.
  - The ears should be clean and clear with no discharge or inflammation.
  - The kitten's stomach may be round but it shouldn't be distended or swollen.
  - The kitten should be able to walk and run normally without any mobility problems.
- Narrow down your options and choose the kitten that you think is the best fit.

Once you've chosen your Teacup Persian kitten, ask the breeder about the next steps. Do not take the kitten home if it isn't at least 8 weeks old and unless it has been fully weaned and eating solid food. Any reputable breeder will not try to sell you a kitten that isn't already weaned or at least 8 weeks old.

Preparing Your Home for a Kitten

Teacup Persians are very gentle and mild-mannered, but all cats have a bit of a mischievous side – especially when they are kittens. You may not be able to stop your Teacup Persian from ever getting into trouble, but you can protect him from getting into things that could hurt him. <u>Preparing your home by kitten-proofing it is very important but also fairly easy to do – just follow these steps:</u>

- Lock up all of your cleaning supplies and other household chemicals in a cupboard or cabinet.

- Place all food in lidded containers or keep it in the pantry – you don't want your cat getting into something that could be bad for him.

- Make sure you don't leave any medications or toiletries out on the counter where you cat could get into them.

- Always unplug electrical cords when they aren't in use and wrap them up so your cat isn't tempted to play with the dangling cord – this is a good idea for blind cords as well.
- Remove any poisonous plants from your home or put them somewhere your cat can't reach them.

- Keep the lid on your toilet seat down so your cat isn't tempted to drink from it – it will also keep a small kitten from accidentally falling in.

- Make sure that your window screens are very secure, especially if your cat is able to jump up into the window.

Always check doorways and appliance doors (like the dryer) before closing them – you never know when your kitten might climb in.

Chapter Four: Caring for Your New Cat

Teacup Persian cats make great family pets, but they do have some specific requirements when it comes to their ideal habitat. This breed is not the most active breed out there, but they do need a lot of attention and their coats require a great deal of grooming. If your cat feels neglected, he may develop problem behaviors or he could even become depressed. In this chapter you will learn the basics about cultivating a safe and happy home for your new cat. You will also receive some tips for picking toys and for keeping your Persian as an indoor or outdoor cat.

Habitat and Exercise Requirements for Teacup Persians

The Persian cat, and therefore the Teacup Persian, is the ultimate lap cat. This is not a cat that you will see running around the house all day, getting into trouble. All cats do have a bit of a mischievous side but, more often than not, your Teacup Persian will be content to sleep the day away – especially if he gets to do it while lying in your lap. Teacup Persians are by no means a high-maintenance breed in terms of their energy level or exercise needs, but they do enjoy human interaction and will revel in every bit of attention that you give them.

Because the Teacup Persian is not an overly active breed, they adapt well to apartment and condo life. These cats also do not tend to jump or climb on things, so your draperies should be safe. Still, you want to make sure that you have plenty of options for your cat to choose from when he is feeling playful. You should also provide your cat with a comfortable place to sleep. Many Teacup Persians enjoy watching the outside world from the comfort of home, so think about installing a shelf at window-level so your cat can watch the birds. Your cat might also appreciate having a plush cat bed to sleep in.

Another factor you need to consider when it comes to the ideal habitat for Teacup Persians is temperature. Teacup Persians have long, double coats that retain a lot of warmth. This being the case, they are very heat sensitive and need to be kept in air conditioning. If your house doesn't have air conditioning, consider installing a window air conditioner in one room where your cat can retreat to if he begins to overheat. You also need to make sure there is plenty of fresh water available at all times.

Toys and Accessories for Teacup Persian Cats

The Teacup Persian is not an overly active breed, but they still enjoy playing – especially kittens. Each cat is unique in terms of what kind of toys he prefers, so start with an assortment and see what your cat likes. Some of the best toys for cats including small balls, wand toys with dangling objects, small mice with rattles or bells inside, and stuffed animals filled with catnip. You can also make your own cat toys using. Many cat owners find that their cats prefer to play with random objects they find around the house instead of the toys they buy them so don't feel like you have to spend a lot on cat toys.

Indoor vs. Outdoor Cats

One of the first questions cat owners get from the veterinarian is whether theirs is an indoor or outdoor cat. Many cats enjoy spending time outdoors because it gives them a chance to roam and they can exercise their hunting skills. There are, however, some potential dangers that come along with letting your cat outside. Not only could he run into predators but he could also be exposed to disease. Outdoor cats need additional vaccinations, so be sure to tell your vet if your Teacup Persian cat goes outside.

If you consult the experts at the American Veterinary Medical Association (AVMA), they will tell you that it is best to keep cats indoors. While cats do have claws and they can be skilled hunters, they are still fairly domesticated and may not be prepared to survive in the outside world. Cats that live indoors only can reach an old age of 17 years or more while outdoor cats live an average of just 5 years. Not only can being outdoors expose your cat to disease and other hazards, but it also reduces the amount of time you spend with him which could mean that it takes you longer to identify behavioral changes or health problems.

When it comes to the Teacup Persian cat specifically, this breed is particularly ill-adapted to outdoor life because their thick, heavy coats make them very sensitive to heat during the summer. Letting your Teacup Persian cat outside might help him to get some extra exercise, but the potential risks are generally not worth it. You should just spend as much time playing with your Teacup Persian indoors as you can to meet his needs for exercise and attention.

Chapter Five: Meeting Your Teacup Persian Cat's Nutritional Needs

Picking out a cat food for your Teacup Persian may seem as simple as walking into a pet store and picking a product off the shelf. What you will find, however, is that there is a huge variety of pet food products out there – how do you know which one will be best for your cat? In this chapter you will learn the basics about the nutritional needs of cats and you will receive tips for choosing a high-quality pet food product for your cat. Keeping your cat healthy is all about nutrition, so read this chapter carefully and take to heart everything you learn!

The Nutritional Needs of Cats

In order to understand the nutritional needs of your Teacup Persian, there is one thing you need to remember – cats are obligate carnivores. This simply means that their bodies are adapted to digest and utilize animal products, not plant products. Whereas dogs are mostly carnivorous but can still tolerate carbohydrates, cats have a very limited ability to digest and absorb nutrients from plant foods. This means that protein – meat – is the most important nutritional consideration for cats. Fat is also important because it provides a concentrated source of energy, but meat is the primary focus.

As you may already know, protein is made up of amino acids and it provides the energy your Teacup Persian cat needs to fuel his healthy growth and development. Protein is important for all cats, but it is particularly important for kittens to help them grow properly. The best proteins for cats come from quality animal sources like meat, poultry, eggs, and fresh fish. These proteins are called complete proteins which means that they contain all of the essential amino acids your cat needs – essential amino acids are simply those that your cat's body is incapable of producing on its own. Plant proteins contain some amino acids, but not all of them

Fat is the second nutritional consideration for cats because it supplies a concentrated source of energy. Fats also contain essential fatty acids that your cat needs for healthy skin, a strong immune system, and nutrient utilization. Again, fats should come from animal sources like chicken fat, salmon oil, or other fish oils instead of plant sources. Your cat should get a balance of omega-3 and omega-6 fatty acids for optimal nutrition.

In addition to protein and fat, cats also need and unlimited supply of fresh water and certain vitamins and minerals. Some of the most important vitamins for cats include fat-soluble vitamins like A, E, D, and K as well as water-soluble vitamins like vitamin C and B vitamins. Minerals that are important for cats include calcium, copper, iodine, manganese, magnesium, potassium, selenium, zinc, and phosphorus. Chelated minerals are the best – these are mineral molecules that have been chemically bonded to protein molecules which makes them easier for your cat's body to digest and absorb.

When it comes to carbohydrates, it is important to note that cats have no nutritional requirement for carbohydrates. They are, however, able to digest certain kinds of carbohydrates in small quantities and they can provide dietary fiber as well as certain essential vitamins and minerals. It important to keep your Teacup Persian cat's carb intake low, however, focusing on higher protein and moderate fat instead.

How to Select a High-Quality Cat Food Brand

For many cat owners, the task of choosing a high-quality cat food can be difficult simply because there are so many different options to choose from. If you walk into your local pet store you will see multiple aisles filled with bags of cat food from different brands and you may also notice that most brands offer a number of different formulas. So how do you choose a healthy at food for your Teacup Persian cat without spending hours at the pet store?

The best place to start when shopping for cat food is to read the cat food label. Pet food in the United States is loosely regulated by the American Association of Feed Control Officials (AAFCO) and they evaluate commercial pet food products according to their ability to meet the basic nutritional needs of cats in various life stages. If the product meets these basic needs, the label will carry some kind of statement from AAFCO like this:

"[Product Name] is formulated to meet the nutritional levels established by the AAFCO Cat Food nutrient profiles for [Life Stage]."

If the cat food product you are looking at contains this statement you can move on to reading the ingredients list. Cat food labels are organized in descending order by volume. This means that the ingredients at the top of the list are used in higher quantities than the ingredients at the end of the list. This being the case, you want to see high-quality sources of animal protein at the beginning of the list because protein is the most important nutrient for cats. Things like fresh meat, poultry or fish are excellent ingredients but they contain about 80% water. After the product is cooked, the actual volume and protein content of the ingredient will be less. Meat meals (like chicken meal or salmon meal) have already been cooked down so they contain up to 300% more protein by weight than fresh meats.

In addition to high-quality animal proteins, you want to check the ingredients list for healthy fats and a limited amount of digestible carbohydrates. In terms of fat, you want to see at least one animal source such as chicken fat or salmon oil. Plant-based fats like flaxseed and canola oil are not necessarily bad, but they are less biologically valuable for your cat. If they are accompanied by an animal source of fat, it is okay. Just make sure that the fats included in the recipe provide a blend of both omega-3 and omega-6 fatty acids. This will help to preserve the quality and condition of your Teacup Persian cat's skin and coat.

For cats, digestible carbohydrates include things like brown rice and oatmeal, as long as they have been cooked properly. You can also look for gluten-free and grain-free options like sweet potato and tapioca. It is best to avoid products that are made with corn, wheat, or soy ingredients because they are low in nutritional value and may trigger food allergies in your cat. You also want to avoid commercial cat foods that contain a large amount of carbohydrates since the cat's body is not adapted to digesting plant materials as effectively as animal products. Cats only need a very small amount of fiber.

In addition to checking the ingredients list for beneficial ingredients you should also know that there are certainly things you do NOT want to see listed. Avoid products made with low-quality fillers like corn gluten meal or rice bran – you should also avoid artificial colors, flavors, and preservatives. Some commonly used artificial preservatives are BHA and BHT. In most cases the label will tell you if natural preservatives are used.

When reading the label for commercial cat food products you need to be careful about taking health claims and marketing gimmicks with a grain of salt. Just because the label includes words like "natural" or "holistic", you cannot make assumptions about what those terms actually mean since the definitions are not regulated for pet foods like they are for people food. That is why you are better off checking for the AAFCO statement of nutritional adequacy and looking at the ingredients list instead of just trusting what the manufacturer says about the product.

Tips for Feeding Your Teacup Persian Cat

When it comes to feeding your Teacup Persian cat you need to be careful about walking the line between feeding him enough to meet his energy needs without feeding him too much. For some cats, you can use an automatic feeder because the cat will self-regulate, eating as much as he needs without overeating. Other cats, however, will eat whatever you put in front of them so you need to ration their daily portion to prevent them from eating too much and becoming overweight or obese.

Another thing you need to be aware of when choosing a cat food for your Teacup Persian is the fact that many cats have a fairly delicate digestive system. Canned cat foods are high in moisture and protein which is good for cats, but they can also be very rich. Rather than feeding your cat a diet that consists entirely of canned food, consider purchasing a high-quality dry food and add a spoonful of wet food on top of it just before feeding. You can also try alternating between dry and canned food for each meal.

Another thing you might want to consider for your Teacup Persian cat is feeding him a raw food diet. The idea of feeding your cat raw meat and bones might sound strange, but it is actually very close to the type of diet wild cats follow – their diets consist almost entirely of whole prey. It is completely natural for cats to eat all parts of their prey including the skin, muscle, organ meats, bones, and connective tissues. If you don't like the idea of preparing raw food for your Teacup Persian you can easily find fresh or frozen raw cat food online and at certain specialty pet stores. Another option is to choose a dehydrated or freeze-dried raw food that can be rehydrated for feeding.

If you aren't sure where to start when shopping for a quality pet food product, you can always refer to pet food review sites. These sites often provide a general breakdown of the top pet food brands, telling you exactly what you want to know about the quality of their ingredients and the safety of their manufacturing processes. These sites also assign ratings for pet food brands based on these criteria. If you are at a loss for what to feed your Teacup Persian, just choose a product that is highly reviewed.

Dangerous Foods to Avoid

It might be tempting to give in to your cat when he is begging at the table, but certain "people foods" can actually be toxic for your cat. As a general rule, you should never feed your cat anything unless you are 100% sure that it is safe. Below you will find a list of foods that can be toxic to cats and should therefore be avoided:

- Alcohol
- Apple seeds
- Avocado
- Cherry pits
- Chocolate
- Coffee

- Garlic
- Grapes/raisins
- Hops
- Macadamia nuts
- Mold
- Mushrooms
- Mustard seeds
- Onions/leeks
- Peach pits
- Potato leaves/stems
- Rhubarb leaves
- Tea
- Tomato leaves/stems
- Walnuts
- Xylitol
- Yeast dough

If your cat eats any of these foods, contact the Pet Poison Control hotline right away at (888) 426 – 4435 to see what you should do next.

Chapter Six: Training Your Teacup Persian

While some cats can learn to do tricks, training a cat is usually very different from training a dog. You can train your cat to use a litterbox and to respond to his name, but some cats simply don't respond as well to training as others. In this chapter you will learn the basics about training and socializing your Teacup Persian kitten including tips for litter training and dealing with problem behaviors. It is a good idea to have a basic understanding of cat training principles before you bring your kitten home so you can deal with problem behaviors as they develop.

Socializing Your New Kitten

Like puppies, kittens are the most impressionable between 8 and 13 weeks of age, though their individual personalities will still be developing for another few months. The Teacup Persian cat is naturally a friendly and outgoing breed, but you still need to socialize your kitten to ensure that he becomes a well-adjusted adult cat. The experiences your kitten has while he is young will impact the way he is as an adult – if you don't give your kitten plenty of new experiences while he is maturing he might respond to new situations as an adult with fear or anxiety.

Fortunately, socialization for Teacup Persian cats is fairly simple – you just have to give your kitten as many new experiences as you can. <u>Here are some simple suggestions for socializing your kitten</u>:

- Introduce your kitten to friends in the comfort of your own home where your kitten feels safe.

- Take your kitten with you to the pet store or to a friend's house so he experiences new locations (don't introduce him to other cats until he is fully vaccinated, however).

- Expose your kitten to people of different sizes, shapes, gender, and skin color.

- Introduce your kitten to children of different ages – just make sure they know how to handle the kitten safely.

- Take your kitten with you in the car when you run errands – just make sure you have a car carrier to keep him safe.

- Make sure your kitten experiences loud noises such as fireworks, cars backfiring, loud music, thunder, etc.

- Introduce your kitten to various appliances and tools such as blenders, lawn mowers, vacuums, etc.

- Play with your kitten using different kinds of toys and experiment with different kinds of food and treats.

Litter Training for Kittens

For the most part, kittens learn to use the litter box from their mothers so you may not have to do any litter training for your Teacup Persian cat at all. You will, however, have to make sure that you teach the kitten the location of the litterbox and give him some time to get used to it. When you bring your kitten home, take your kitten to the litter box and place him inside. He may scratch around a little bit or he might jump right out – either is fine. Just keep putting your kitten in the litter box a few times a day for the first few days until he gets used to the location. You should also make sure that it is in a quiet, easy to reach location.

If you have more than one Teacup Persian cat, you should also have more than one litter box. The best rule of thumb to follow is one litterbox per cat plus one extra. Some cats do not mind sharing litterboxes but others will refuse to use one that another cat has used. Some cats also use one litterbox to urinate and another to defecate. Set up your litterboxes in a quiet, private place that is easy to access. If you have a dog in the house you may need to place the box somewhere he can't get to it – some dogs will eat clumps out of the litterbox.

There are many different types of litter boxes to choose from so you have plenty of options. Just be sure that the box you choose is large enough for your cat to get into and move around in easily. In terms of the type of litter, most cats prefer fine-textured litter to coarse litter. You should keep about 2 inches of litter in the box at all times and scoop it frequently and refresh it with new litter. It is usually best to keep less litter in the box and to clean it more often than to use a lot of litter. Just be careful not to choose a litter that is too dusty or one that has too much fragrance added to it – these things could aggravate allergies in your Teacup Persian cat.

Dealing with Problem Behaviors

Teacup Persian cats are smart but they are not very active when compared to other breeds. This is generally a good thing because if you have a cat that is both smart and highly active, there is a high risk that he will find ways to get into trouble. Even though Teacup Persians don't need a lot of exercise, if your cat doesn't get the attention he needs, he could become destructive in the house or he might develop other problem behaviors like urinating outside the litter box or scratching the furniture.

The Teacup Persian cat is a very smart breed and he will always be paying attention to you when you spend time together – he will take his cues from you and watch how you react to the things he does. If your cat does something you don't like, you should not punish him for it. It is very unlikely that your cat will connect the punishment to the crime and he might just end up being afraid of you. Instead, you need to either teach your cat that bad behaviors don't earn him the attention he wants or you should provide a more suitable outlet for the behavior.

When it comes to things like scratching, you should not try to completely eradicate this behavior. Scratching is a normal and important behavior for cats because it helps them to stretch their toes and to spread their scent through glands in the pads of their feet. If your Teacup Persian cat is scratching up your furniture, the solution may be as simple as providing him with scratching posts around the house. To encourage your cat to use them instead of your furniture, sprinkle them with dried catnip or use a liquid catnip spray. When your cat uses the scratching post, give him a couple of treats as well to encourage him.

Teacup Persians have very large, expressive eyes and they use them to communicate with you – these cats do not tend to be very vocal. If your particular cat does develop a tendency to meow for attention, you should not try to eliminate the behavior completely. You can, however, reduce annoying behaviors like incessant meowing by not giving in to your cat. If he meows at you for attention and you give it to him, you will only be reinforcing that behavior. If you want your cat to leave you alone while you are working on the computer, for example, just ignore him until he gives up. Eventually your cat will learn when it is play time and when it is not.

Chapter Seven: Grooming Your Persian

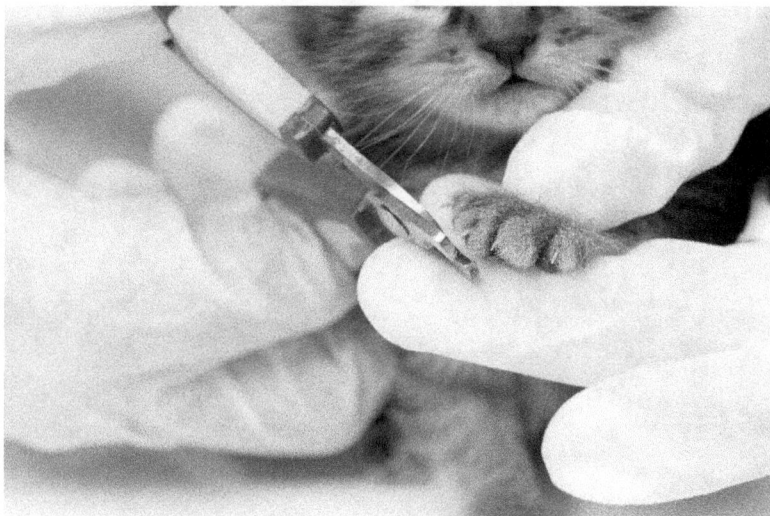

The Persian Cat (and the Teacup Persian) is known for its long, luxurious coat. As beautiful as this coat is, it requires a lot of maintenance to keep it looking and feeling its best. In this chapter you will learn the basics about grooming your Teacup Persian including a list of recommended tools, tips for brushing and bathing your cat, and information about other grooming tasks such as trimming your cat's nails and cleaning his ears.

Recommended Tools to Have on Hand

In order to keep your Teacup Persian's coat and skin in good condition, you will need to brush and bathe him on a regular basis. It is best to brush your cat's coat at least once a day but you can choose whether you want to bathe him yourself or send him to a professional groomer. <u>If you groom you cat yourself, you will need these supplies</u>:

- Wide-toothed comb
- Wire-pin brush
- Slicker brush
- Undercoat rake
- Cat-friendly shampoo

- Cat nail trimmers
- Cat ear cleaner
- Cotton balls or swabs
- Cat toothbrush
- Cat toothpaste

Tips for Bathing and Grooming Teacup Persian Cats

To keep your Teacup Persian cat's coat and skin in good condition, you should plan to brush him at least once a day. To begin, use a wide-toothed comb and gently go over your cat's entire body (especially the armpits and behind his ears) to check for tangles and mats. If you come across a tangle or a mat, try to use your fingers to work through it, using the teeth of the comb if necessary. If the mat or tangle is too severe and you absolutely can't work it out, you can cut it out. Pinch the hair below the mat as close to your cat's skin as you can with your thumb and forefinger. Then, with a pair of sharp scissors, cut a few hairs at a time until you can pull the mat free.

After removing any mats and tangles from your Teacup Persian's coat you should use a wire pin brush or a slicker brush to go over his coat once more to remove dead hairs. When brushing your cat, be sure to always brush in the direction of hair growth and go slowly. Start at the base of your cat's head, working your way down the neck and along his back and sides. Don't forget his legs, chest, and tail, either! Keep an eye out for tangles and mats you may have missed as you go along.

Though cats generally do a good job of keeping themselves clean, you may still need to bathe your Teacup Persian every two to six weeks to keep his coat clean and shiny. When bathing your Teacup Persian, it is essential that you choose the right shampoo for your cat's coat color. For white-coated cats choose a clear, white, or brightening shampoo. For black Persians, choose a darkening shampoo. Red tabby Persians need red in their shampoo and dilutes and bi-color cats need a shampoo that suits their dominant color and brightens their whites.

When you are ready to bathe your cat, fill the sink or bathtub with a few inches of warm water then use your hand or a cup to dampen your cat's fur. Be careful not to get his face, eyes, or ears wet as you do so. Just a little bit of shampoo and work it into a lather in your cat's coat then rinse it thoroughly to remove all soap residue with warm water. Once your cat is clean, use a towel to remove excess moisture then carefully blow-dry his coat on the cool or low heat setting and brush it well.

Other Grooming Tasks

In addition to brushing and bathing your Teacup Persian cat, you also need to engage in some other grooming tasks including trimming your cat's nails, cleaning his ears, and brushing his teeth. You will find an overview of each of these grooming tasks below:

Trimming Your Cat's Nails

Your cat's nails grow in the same way that your own nails grow so they need to be trimmed occasionally. Most cat owners find that trimming their cat's nails once a week or twice a month is sufficient. Before you trim your Teacup Persian cat's nails for the first time you should have your veterinarian or a professional groomer show you how to do it. A cat's nail contains a quick – the blood vessel that supplies blood to the nail – and if you cut the nail too short you could sever it. A severed quick will cause your cat pain and it will bleed profusely. The best way to avoid cutting your cat's nails too short is to just trim the sharp tip.

Cleaning Your Cat's Ears

The Teacup Persian has fairly small ears and they are open which reduces the risk for moisture getting trapped inside. Still, you should make an effort to keep them clean to prevent wax buildup. To clean your cat's ears, use a cat ear cleaning solution and squeeze a few drops into the ear canal. Then, massage the base of your cat's ears to distribute the solution then wipe it away using a clean cotton ball.

Brushing Your Cat's Teeth

You will learn more about periodontal disease in Teacup Persian cats later in this book but for now you should know that keeping your cat's teeth clean is very important. Many cat owners neglect their cat's dental health which is a serious mistake. Brushing your cat's teeth is fairly easy, though you will need a special pet toothbrush and pet toothpaste to do it – you may also need to get your cat accustomed to the toothbrush and the tooth-brushing process slowly. Ideally you should be brushing your cat's teeth every day but if he will only let you do it a few times a week then that is certainly better than nothing.

Chapter Eight: Breeding Your Teacup Persian Cat

Persian cats are a beautiful and loving breed which is why they are so popular among pet owners and breeders. These cats can fetch high prices as well, which is another draw for some people. But if your only motivation for breeding your Teacup Persian is to make money, please reconsider. Breeding cats is by no means a simple task and it is more expensive than you might realize – many breeders are lucky to break even after covering the veterinary costs for their pregnant female and initial exams and vaccinations for the kittens. If you are considering breeding your cat, keep the information in this chapter in mind and do more of your own research to be sure you really understand the risks before you set out to breed your cat.

Basic Cat Breeding Information

Before you decide whether or not to breed your Teacup Persian cat, you should understand the basics of cat breeding so that you know what you are getting yourself into. The idea of having a litter of cute and cuddly kittens to play with might sound great, but can you dedicate the time and money to raising those kittens until they are old enough to go to new homes? And what will you do if your pregnant cat has complications during her pregnancy?

Another thing you need to think about before breeding Teacup Persians is the fact that this breed is prone to a number of serious hereditary health problem such as polycystic kidney disease (PKD), hypertrophic cardiomyopathy, progressive retinal atrophy, and liver shunts. Before you even think about breeding cats you need to have your breeding stock (both the male and female cat) DNA tested to ensure that they aren't carriers for any one of these diseases. You may also need to register yourself as a cattery if you want to register your litter with TICA or with the CFA. These are just a few of the things to think about before you really decide to breed your cat.

If you are able to jump through the preliminary hoops for registering your cats and your cattery, you can then start thinking about the actual breeding process for Teacup Persian cats. Female cats in general can go into heat as early as 6 months of age. Heat is another name for the estrus cycle which is the female cat's reproductive cycle during which she becomes receptive to mating. If a female cat in heat is mated to an intact male during her cycle, there is a possibility that she will become pregnant.

The heat cycle in cats typically lasts between 1 and 3 weeks, depending on whether the cat is bred or not. Cats are seasonally polyestrus animals which means that they can have multiple heat cycles throughout the breeding season. In the Northern Hemisphere, most cats cycle between January and September. If you live in a tropical region, your cat could cycle all year round. The actual heat cycle can last as little as 1 day or as long as 7 days. If the cat is not mated, she will go out of heat for a period of 1 to 2 weeks, making the entire estrus cycle last a total of up to 3 weeks.

It is not difficult to tell when a female cat goes into heat. You may not notice any vaginal discharge (one of the first physical signs of heat) but you will notice some behavioral changes. Your Persian cat might become even more affectionate than usual, rubbing herself on you or on household objects and rolling on the floor. Persian cats can also become quite vocal while they are in heat. Some female cats also urinate more often during heat or they can spray urine as a means of marking their territory.

If you plan to breed your Persian cat then you need to know when is the best time to try to get her pregnant. What is unique about cats is that they are "induced ovulators" – this means that the female cat will not actually ovulate until she is mated to a male cat. The act of mating stimulates the release of eggs from the ovaries so, while the cat can technically become pregnant at any time during her cycle, it may take multiple matings within a single 24-hour period for her to actually conceive. Semen can also remain in the cat's reproductive system for several days and a single litter of kittens can have multiple fathers.

Breeding Tips and Raising Kittens

It is entirely possible for your Teacup Persian female cat to become pregnant during her first heat cycle, but most breeders recommend waiting until she is at least 1 year old – many even recommend waiting until she is 18 to 24 months old. The first heat cycle signals that the cat is sexually mature, but she may still be growing and the stress of a pregnancy could impact her development. Male cats usually reach sexual maturity between 8 and 9 months of aged but you should wait until he is about 18 months old to breed him. This will give you time to determine his temperament and to see whether any hereditary conditions manifest.

If you successfully mate your Teacup Persian cats and the female becomes pregnant, she will enter a gestation period that generally lasts about 63 days. It is important to keep track of when you bred your cat so you can predict her due date and keep an eye on her throughout the pregnancy. You will not be able to tell right away that your cat is pregnant but about two weeks after conception you may start to notice some pinking in the nipple area. After 25 to 30 days you may be able to actually feel the kittens inside her, but be very careful because you don't want to hurt them. X-rays can be used to confirm pregnancy and to count the kittens after about 38 days and ultrasound can be used as early as 14 but it is most accurate after 28 days. The average litter size for Teacup Persian cats is between 1 and 9 kittens, though most litters are between 3 and 5.

When your Teacup Persian cat nears the end of the gestation period you should provide her with a nesting box in which to whelp (birth) the kittens. This box should be placed in a quiet, dark area and you should line it with old towels or blankets that you can throw out after the birth. Some of the signs that your cat will give birth soon may include panting or labored breathing, persistent licking of the abdominal area, pelvic contractions, loss of appetite, pacing the room, vocalizations. Once your Teacup Persian cat begins to give birth, the whole litter should be delivered within 2 to 3 hours. After all the kittens are born, the mother will bite off the umbilical cords and clean them.

It is very important that your Teacup Persian kittens start to nurse soon after birth because the first milk the mother produces contains essential nutrients and antibodies that will protect the kittens while their own immune systems are developing – this first milk is called colostrum. Persian kittens usually weigh between 3 and 3.5 ounces (80 to 100 grams) at birth, so you can expect your Teacup Persian kittens to be a little smaller. Kittens are born with their eyes and ears closed so they are completely dependent on their mothers for warmth and food – the mother cat will also lick them to stimulate their breathing.

For the first two weeks, your Teacup Persian kittens will do little but sleep and nurse. Their eyes will open after 8 to 12 days and they will start orienting themselves to sound as well. After 3 weeks the kittens become a little more active, spending more time playing and less time nursing. After four weeks the kittens should start playing with toys and using the litter box – their baby teeth will also start to develop and they may start sampling solid food. A Teacup Persian kitten's sight is fully developed after 5 to 6 weeks and they will learn grooming skills from their mother after about 7 weeks.

Between 8 and 13 weeks, your Teacup Persian kittens will need a lot of socialization. The mother should naturally start weaning them after 6 weeks or so and they should be fully weaned by 8 weeks. During this time, kittens are highly impressionable and you want to expose them to as many new things as possible to ensure that they are properly socialized. By 14 weeks your Teacup Persian kittens should be weaned, socialized, litter trained, and ready to be separated from their mother and sent to their new homes.

Chapter Nine: Showing Your Teacup Persian Cat

The Persian is by far one of the most beautiful cat breeds out there and also one of the most popular breeds for show. Unfortunately, the Teacup Persian has not been recognized as a separate breed and it does not meet the size requirements for CFA or TICA shows. Even though you may not be able to enter your Teacup Persian into one of these official shows, you may still be able to find shows sponsored by local or regional breed clubs. In this chapter you will find an overview of the CFA and TICA Persian breed standard as well as tips for showing your cat.

Persian Cat Breed Standard

As it has already been mentioned, the Teacup Persian is not eligible for show with the CFA or TICA due to its small size. If you have your heart set on showing your Teacup Persian, however, you may be able to find local cat shows that have more lax regulations. You can also check with your local breed club or cat fanciers organization for ideas. To give you an idea what your cat should look like if you want to show him, consider both the CFA and TICA standards for the Persian breed.

a.) CFA Breed Standard

General

The breed is heavy boned but well-balanced with soft, rounded lines and a sweet expression. The cat has large, round eyes set wide apart in a large, round head. The long, thick coat softens the lines and accentuates the roundness.

Head and Ears

The head is round and massive, the skull having great breadth. The face is round, the head well set on a short, thick neck. When viewed in profile, the eyes are prominent and the chin, nose, and forehead are in vertical alignment. The nose is short, the cheeks full, and the jaws broad and powerful. The ears are small and round-tipped, tilted forward and set low on the head. The eyes are brilliant in color, large, and round.

Body and Legs

The body is of cobby type, low on the legs, the chest broad. The cat has good muscle tone without being obese and is medium or large in size. The legs are short, thick, and strong with large, round paws and toes carried close – there are five in front and four in back. The tail is proportionate to body length and carried without curve.

Coat, Skin and Color

The coat is long and thick, standing well away from the body. It has a fine texture and is long all over the body, including the shoulders. There is a ruff around the neck and a deep frill between the legs. For tabby cats, 20 points are divided evenly between marking and color. For bi-color cats, 20 points are divided evenly between color and pattern.

Penalties and Disqualifications

Kinked or abnormal tail; incorrect number of toes; weakness in the hindquarters; any deformity of the spine or skull; crossed eyes.

Summary of Points:

Below you will find a summary of points to which Persian cats are compared in judging. All three categories add up to a total of 100 possible points.

Head (30 points)

- Size/Shape of Eyes

- Ear Shape and Set
- Nose and Cheeks

Body Type (20 points)

- Body Shape
- Overall Size
- Body/Bone
- Length of Tail

Coat (10 points)

Balance (5 points)

Refinement (5 points)

Color (20 points)

Eye Color (10 points)

b.) TICA Breed Standard

General

The ideal specimen of the breed is strong and well-balanced with excellent boning and musculature. The cat gives the impression of robust power with a pleasant expression. It is well-balanced both physically and temperamentally, and amenable to handling.

Head and Ears

The head is round, broad and smooth-domed – it is medium to large in size, proportionate to the body. The jaws are broad and powerful, cheeks full and prominent, the eyes sweet of expression. The ears are small and round-tipped, set wide apart. The eyes are round, full, and large, set level and far apart – deep, brilliant color is preferred. The chin is strong and full, the muzzle short and the profile short and snub-nose. The forehead, nose and chin are in a straight line, the neck short and thick.

Body and Legs

The torso is cobby with a well-rounded midsection, medium to large in size. The boning is heavy, the musculature firm and well-developed. The back is level, the chest deep, and the abdomen well-rounded. The legs are large of bone and well-muscled, short and straight from the breadth of the chest. The feet are large and round, the tail short and straight but in proportion to body length.

Coat, Skin and Color

The coat is long all over the body and full of life. The dense undercoat gives great volume and the ruff is immense. Clear color is preferred with subtle shading allowed – allowances are also made for darker shaded areas in mature cats. There should be contrast between the body and point color with points falling on the ears, legs, feet, tail and mask.

Penalties and Disqualifications

Long or narrow head, long Roman nose, or thin muzzle; missing canine teeth; asymmetry (should be penalized in proportion with severity); ears that are large, pointed, or too close together; narrow chest or long back; poor muscle tone or coat condition; pale, weak color. Kinked tail; severe malocclusion or asymmetric facial structure; severe undershot or overshot jaw.

Summary of Points:

Below you will find a summary of points to which Persian cats are compared in judging. All three categories add up to a total of 100 possible points.

Head (35 points)

- Size/Shape – 5 points
- Ears – 5 points
- Eyes – 10 points
- Chin – 3 points

- Nose – 5 points
- Profile – 5 points
- Neck – 2 points

Body (35 points)

- Neck – 5 points
- Chest – 10 points
- Abdomen and Rump – 10 points
- Legs and Feet – 5 points
- Tail – 5 points

Coat/Color/Pattern (20 points)

- Length/Texture – 10 points
- Color/Pattern – 10 points

Other (10 points)

- Condition – 5 points
- Balance – 5 points

Preparing Your Teacup Persian Cat for Show

Although you may not be able to show your Teacup Persian at an official CFA or TICA show, you may be able to find other local or regional cat shows in your area. The rules and regulations will vary from one show to another, so do your research beforehand to make sure that your cat is a good specimen for show. In addition to comparing your cat to the Persian breed standard, there are some general things you can do to prepare for a cat show.

Below you will find a list of general tips and tricks to help prepare you and your cat for show:

- Make sure your cat is properly pedigreed according to the regulations of the show – you may need to present your cat's papers as proof so have them ready.

- You may have the option of showing your Teacup Persian cat in the pet category for some shows – if you choose this option, be sure to read the unique standard requirements for that category.

- Make sure to fill out the registration form correctly, providing all of the necessary details, and turn it in on time – you may also have to pay an entry fee at this time as well.

- Clip your Teacup Persian cat's claws before the show – declawed cats are allowed as well without penalty.
- Make sure that your cat is registered with the organization running the show.

- Be sure to enter your cat in the proper age bracket or category - some organizations allow kittens as young as 3 months of age.

- Find out what is provided by the show and what you need to bring yourself – some competitions provide an exhibition cage but you will need to bring some things.

In order to make sure that you are fully prepared for the show, pack and bring the following things:

- Your cat's pedigree and registration papers.
- Veterinary records and proof of vaccinations.
- Litter pan and cat litter (if not provided).
- Food, treats, and food/water bowls.
- Cage curtains and clips to hang them.
- A blanket or bed for the cage.
- Any necessary grooming equipment, nail clippers.
- Confirmation slip received at entry.
- Food, water, and extra clothes for yourself.
- Garbage bag for clean-up.

Be prepared to spend all day at the show and bring with you everything you and your cat need to make it through the day. Some shows provide a list of recommended materials to bring so pay close attention to all of the information the show gives you with your registration.

Chapter Ten: Keeping Your Cat Healthy

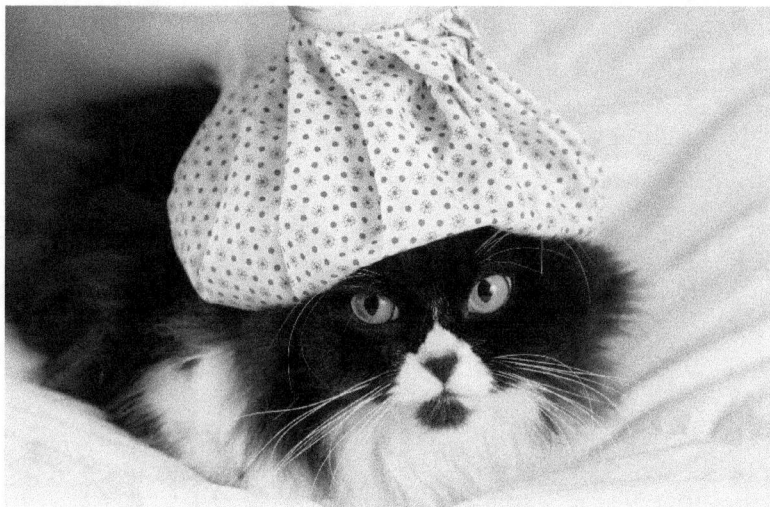

It won't take long for your Teacup Persian cat to become your loyal friend and companion, so it should be a no-brainer that you will do what it takes to keep your friend happy and healthy for as long as possible. While feeding your cat a healthy diet is a great way to maintain his health, you cannot always prevent your cat from getting a disease simply by watching what he eats. All cats are prone to certain diseases so the responsible thing to do is learn about the conditions to which the Teacup Persian is prone so you can keep an eye out.

Common Health Problems Affecting Teacup Persians

In this section you will receive an overview of some of the conditions most commonly affecting the Teacup Persian cat breed. By educating yourself about the causes, symptoms, and treatment for these common conditions you can help to keep your cat in good health for as long as possible. Some of the common conditions affecting Persian cats (including Teacup Persians) include:

- Bladder Stones
- Cystitis
- Dental Malocclusions
- Hypertrophic Cardiomyopathy
- Liver Shunts

- Periodontal Disease
- Polycystic Kidney Disease
- Progressive Retinal Atrophy
- Seborrhea Oleosa

In addition to these health conditions, Persian cats are also particularly sensitive to heat due to the thickness and density of their coats. These cats do not do well as outdoor cats and they need to be kept in air conditioning in the hotter temperatures of summer.

Bladder Stones

Bladder stones are made up of microscopic crystals which, though generally very small, can become large enough to block the urethra in male cats, preventing the cat from being able to urinate. Bladder stones can technically form anywhere in the urinary tract – they can even be found in the kidneys, bladder, urethra, or the ureters (the tubes that carry urine from the kidneys to the bladder). In many cases, cats with bladder stones urinate frequently but only pass a small amount of urine and it may be tinged with blood. Cats may also strain or cry out in pain when urinating.

Bladder stones are made up of magnesium, phosphate, and ammonium so dietary changes to reduce these minerals may be helpful. If the stones become too large to pass normally, surgical removal may be necessary. To prevent the stones from reforming you may need to make some changes to your cat's diet and you might need to feed him several small meals throughout the day instead of one or two large meals. Increasing your cat's water consumption is also very important so make sure he keeps drinking water throughout the day and consider switching him over to a canned food diet.

Cystitis

Also known as bladder inflammation, cystitis is a chronic disease that can be tricky to treat. This condition usually causes symptoms typically associated with lower urinary tract disease such as frequent urination, straining to urinate, crying during urination, urinating in inappropriate places, and blood in the urine. The cause for this condition is not completely understood, though it is generally thought that stress plays a role. It may also be related to abnormalities in the cat's cardiovascular, nervous, and endocrine systems.

Because the symptoms of cystitis overlap with those of lower urinary tract disease, diagnosis can sometimes be tricky. Some of the tests your veterinarian might perform include complete blood cell count, urinalysis, and an abdominal x-ray. Treatment for this condition usually involves environmental changes to reduce your cat's stress level as well as dietary modifications and medications for pain. Increased water consumption is usually very helpful, so make sure your cat drinks plenty of water and consider switching him to a canned food diet.

Dental Malocclusions

Not only are Persian and Teacup Persian cats prone to periodontal disease, but there are other dental problems that can be caused by their compressed facial structure. The crowding of their teeth actually adds to the risk for periodontal disease because bacteria can accumulate in gaps between the teeth. Many Teacup Persians also experience dental malocclusions, or malpositioned teeth. Sometimes the teeth look loose or crooked – they may also protrude into the opposite gums or lips.

In most cases, the signs of dental malocclusions develop between 14 and 24 weeks of age as the cat's teeth start to grow in. As long as the overcrowding isn't painful for your cat and it doesn't cause excessive wear and tear, no treatment is necessary besides regular brushing to keep the teeth clean and professional cleanings to remove plaque and tartar. If the condition becomes painful, however, it may be necessary to extract non-strategic teeth.

Hypertrophic Cardiomyopathy

Your cat's heart has four chambers – two at the top and two at the bottom. The left ventricle (on the bottom of the heart) is responsible for taking oxygenated blood from the lungs and sending it through the aortic valve (the main artery in the body) to other body parts. For cats with hypertrophic cardiomyopathy (HCM), however, the muscle of the left ventricle becomes thickened and enlarged which may affect its ability to function properly. This condition is very common in cat between 5 and 7 years of age as well as certain breeds. It is generally considered to be the most common form of heart disease in cats.

The cause of hypertrophic cardiomyopathy in cats is unknown in many cases, though there is thought to be a genetic component. Cats with hypertension or hyperthyroidism also seem to have a higher risk for developing HCM. Some of the most common symptoms of this condition include loss of appetite, lethargy, difficulty breathing, weak pulse, abnormal heart rhythm, exercise intolerance, limb paralysis, collapse, and heart failure. Treatment options for HCM depend on the severity of the condition and may include medical treatments to slow the heart rate and to improve blood flow. Keeping your cat on a sodium-restricted diet may also be a part of his long-term treatment plan along with a low-stress environment.

Liver Shunts

Also known as portosystemic shunt, liver shunts can be an inherited condition in Persian and Teacup Persian cats. Also known as PSS, a portosystemic shunt an abnormality in the portal vein. The portal vein is the vein that transports blood from the circulatory system to the liver for filtration. A portosystemic shunt occurs when an abnormality forms between the portal vein and another vein, causing blood to bypass the liver. Without proper filtration of the blood, the cat may develop symptoms like stunted growth, poor muscle development, behavioral changes, and seizures.

In order to diagnose your cat with portosystemic shunt, your veterinarian will perform an exam and a medical history. He may also order tests like a complete blood count, urinalysis, and a bile acid test. With medication and dietary changes, most cats with portosystemic shunt improve quickly. For those that don't, however, surgery may be required to repair the defect. In some cases, antibiotics are prescribed and lactulose might be needed to help reduce toxin absorption in the body. Most cats that do require surgery for portosystemic shunt live long, healthy lives – the survival rate is very high.

Periodontal Disease

If you think that brushing your cat's teeth sounds silly, you may want to rethink your position. Periodontal disease (or gum disease) is incredibly common in cats and it can be very serious. For humans, the most common dental problem is cavities but, for cats, it is gingivitis – a buildup of plaque around or under the gum line. If left untreated, this condition can progress to serious periodontal disease. It could start damaging the tooth or the underlying skeletal structure and bacteria could also leech into the bloodstream, causing a systemic infection.

When it comes to dental disease in cats, there are a number of contributing factors. Normal tartar buildup is simply due to food particles and bacteria accumulating on the surface of the teeth. In some cases, however, dental problems can be secondary to another type of disease or infection. For example, feline leukemia virus and feline immunodeficiency virus can contribute to dental problems in cats like the Teacup Persian. You will need to have your cat examined by a vet in order to confirm the condition and to decide on the treatment. In some cases it may be necessary to put the cat under general anesthesia for a deep cleaning and to remove any damaged or infected teeth.

Polycystic Kidney Disease

This is a kind of progressive, inherited disease characterized by numerous cysts forming in the cat's kidneys. This condition is present at birth and the cysts usually begin very small in size but they gradually grow in size as the cat matures. As the cysts get larger, they can impact kidney function and eventually lead to kidney failure. In most cases, Teacup Persian cats are between 3 and 10 years old when symptoms first develop. The most common signs include weight loss, decreased appetite, poor coat condition, increased thirst and urination and dehydration.

Unfortunately, polycystic kidney disease cannot be cured and the progression cannot be stopped. The best thing to do for your cat is to offer supportive therapies to improve his quality of life as much as possible. Making dietary changes to stimulate appetite and to reduce stress on the kidneys is very important and hormone therapy can sometimes help to balance out the cat's calcium and phosphorus ratios. In cases where the can becomes anemic, injections may be used to regenerate blood cells. With treatment some cats live long lives – especially those who receive a kidney transplant – but most cats ultimately succumb to death from kidney failure.

Progressive Retinal Atrophy

Also known as PRA, progressive retinal atrophy is generally not as common in cats as in dogs, but it is an inherited condition in the Persian breed. PRA affects the retina of the eye, the part that receives light and converts it into electrical nerve signals that the brain interprets as vision. Cats with PRA typically experience arrested retinal development (called retina dysplasia) or early degeneration of the photoreceptors in the eye. Cats with retinal dysplasia usually develop symptoms within 2 months and are often blind by 3 to 5 years of age.

The signs of PRA vary according to the rate of progression. This disease is not painful and it doesn't affect the outward appearance of the eye. In most cases, cat owners notice a change in the cat's willingness to go down stairs, or to go down a dark hallway – PRA causes night blindness which can progress to total blindness. Unfortunately, there is no treatment or cure for progressive retinal atrophy and no way to slow the progression of the disease. Most cats with PRA eventually become blind.

Seborrhea Oleosa

Also known as seborrhea dermatitis, this is a skin condition in dogs that affects the sebaceous glands. These glands are located in the skin along the dog's back and they are responsible for producing sebum. The most common signs of this disease include flaking skin (dandruff), areas of red and inflamed skin, and the formation of dry or oily lesions. The areas most commonly affected include the feet, armpits, thighs, underside, neck and lips. Many dogs with seborrhea dermatitis also develop an odor.

The exact cause for seborrhea dermatitis cannot always be determined, though it is often related to an underlying medical problem such as thyroid disease, parasite infections, fungal infections, obesity, or musculoskeletal disease. It could also be related to environmental factors like humidity or temperature changes as well as seasonal allergies. Treating the underlying cause is usually the most effective treatment but other therapies that might help include fatty acid supplements, antiseborrheic shampoo baths, topical moisturizers, and antibiotics.

Preventing Illness with Vaccinations

Feeding your cat a healthy diet is a good way to maintain his overall health, but there are still some diseases that could threaten his wellbeing if you aren't careful. Fortunately, there are vaccines available for a number of these conditions. While your kitten is still young he may need several doses of certain vaccines and then, once he reaches adulthood, he can cut back to annual boosters. Your veterinarian will be able to tell you which vaccines your cat needs and when he needs them.

One thing you need to know about vaccines for cats is that they are divided into two categories: core and non-core. Core vaccines are those that are recommended for all cats and they include panleukopenia (feline distemper), feline calicivirus, feline herpes virus type I (rhinotracheitis) and rabies. Non-core vaccines are recommended for certain cats depending on certain risk factors such as location and lifestyle. Non-core vaccines may include feline leukemia virus (FeLV) for outdoor cats and Chlamydophila for cats that have been exposed to the virus.

To give you an idea what kind of vaccinations your kitten will need, consult the vaccination schedule on the following page:

Vaccine	First Vaccination	Booster Shots
Core Vaccines		
Panleukopenia	6 weeks; every 3 weeks after until 16 weeks	1 dose second year then once every 3 years
Rhinotracheitis	6 weeks; every 3 weeks after until 16 weeks	1 dose second year then once every 3 years
Calcivirus	6 weeks; every 3 weeks after until 16 weeks	1 dose second year then once every 3 years
Feline Herpes Virus I	6 weeks; every 3 weeks after until 16 weeks	1 dose second year then once every 3 years
Rabies (not in the UK)	single dose, as early as 8 weeks	Annually or every 3 years, depending on type of vaccine
Non-Core Vaccines		
Feline Leukemia	as early as 8 weeks, again 3 -4 weeks later	annual
Chlamydophila	as needed	as needed
Feline Infectious Peritonitis	as needed	as needed

Bordatella	as early as 8 weeks, again 2 -4 weeks later	annual
Giardia	as needed	as needed

** Keep in mind that vaccine requirements may vary from one region to another. Only your vet will be able to tell you which vaccines are most important for the region where you live.

Teacup Persian Cat Care Sheet

As you read through this book you received a wealth of information about the Persian and Teacup Persian cat breeds. Not only will this information help to prepare you for cat ownership, but it will continue to be a useful resource for you throughout the life of your cat. As you and your Teacup Persian cat get used to each other you may find that you need to reference certain bits of information from this book. Rather than flipping through the entire book to find what you need, use this care sheet to reference key facts and tidbits about the Teacup Persian cat breed.

1.) Basic Teacup Persian Cat Information

Pedigree: same breed as the Persian cat but selectively bred down in size for Teacup variety

Breed Size: small

Weight: 3 to 5 pounds for females, up to 8 pounds for males

Coat Length: long

Coat Texture: very soft, silky and luxurious

Color: comes in a wide variety of solid and bi-color patterns including Himalayan, tabby, tortoiseshell, and more

Eyes and Nose: eyes are large and round, color is usually copper or blue; nose color varies by coloration

Ears: small with rounded tips

Tail: long and plumed

Temperament: gentle, quiet, laidback, lazy, affectionate, people-oriented, loving

Strangers: typically warms up quickly

Children: generally patient as long as the child knows how to properly handle a cat; may not tolerate rough handling

Other Pets: can do well when raised together

Exercise Needs: fairly low

Health Conditions: polycystic kidney disease (PKD), hypertrophic cardiomyopathy, progressive retinal atrophy, liver shunts, cystitis, bladder stones, eye conditions, dental malocclusions, seborrhea oleosa

Lifespan: 10 to 15 years average

2.) Basic Cat Nutritional Needs

Nutritional Needs: water, protein, carbohydrate, fats, vitamins, minerals

Calorie Needs: varies by age, weight, and activity level

Amount to Feed (kitten): feed freely but consult recommendations on the package

Amount to Feed (adult): consult recommendations on the package; calculated by weight

Feeding Frequency: two meals daily

Important Ingredients: fresh animal protein (chicken, beef, lamb, turkey, eggs), animal fats, digestible carbohydrates (rice, oats, sweet potato)

Important Minerals: calcium, copper, iodine, manganese, magnesium, potassium, selenium, zinc, and phosphorus

Important Vitamins: Vitamin A, Vitamin C, Vitamin B, Vitamin D, Vitamin E, Vitamin K

Look For: AAFCO statement of nutritional adequacy; protein at top of ingredients list; no artificial flavors, dyes, preservatives

3.) Cat Breeding Information

Sexual Maturity (female): average 5 to 6 months

Sexual Maturity (male): 8 to 9 months

Breeding Age (female): 12 months, ideally 18 to 24 months

Breeding Age (male): at least 18 months

Breeding Type: seasonally polyestrous, multiple cycles per year

Ovulation: induced ovulation, stimulated by breeding

Litter Size: 1 to 9 kittens, average 3 to 5

Pregnancy: average 63 days

Kitten Birth Weight: 3 to 3.5 ounces (80 to 100 grams)

Characteristics at Birth: eyes and ears closed, little to no fur, completely dependent on mother

Eyes/Ears Open: 8 to 12 days

Teeth Grow In: around 3 to 4 weeks

Begin Weaning: around 4 to 6 weeks, kittens are fully weaned by 8 weeks

Socialization: between 8 and 13 weeks, ready to be separated by 14 weeks

Index

C

D

E

F

G

H

I

J

K

L

R

S

T

U

V

W

References

"About the Persian." The Cat Fanciers Association.
   <http://cfa.org/Breeds/BreedsKthruR/Persian.aspx>

"Basic Cat Training." Love That Pet.
   <https://www.lovethatpet.com/cats/behaviour-and-
   training/cat-training-tips/>

"Bladder Inflammation in Cats." PetMD.
   <http://www.petmd.com/cat/conditions/urinary/c_ct_bla
   dder_inflammation_feline_interstitial_cystitis?page=2>

"Cat Breeding." PetEducation.com.
   <http://www.peteducation.com/article.cfm?c=1+2139&aid
   =891>

"Cat Nutrition Tips." ASPCA. <http://www.aspca.org/pet-
   care/cat-care/cat-nutrition-tips>

"Glossary of Feline Terms." Cat World. <http://www.cat-
   world.com.au/glossary>

"Grooming a Persian Cat." Purrinlot.
   <http://www.purrinlot.com/grooming-help.htm>

"How Often Should You Feed Your Cat?" Cornell University
   College of Veterinary Medicine.
   <http://www.vet.cornell.edu/fhc/Health_Information/CW
   _Feed.cfm>

"How to Mate a Persian Cat." Cuteness.com.
    <https://www.cuteness.com/article/mate-persian-cat>

"Hybrid Cats: Alaskan Snow Cat." Ultimate Cat.
    <http://ultimatecat.blogspot.com/2011/06/hybrid-cats-
    alaskan-snow-cat.html>

King, Marcia. "Persian Cat Genetic Disease."
    CatChannel.com. <http://www.catchannel.com/about-
    persian/persian-health-problems.aspx>

"Persian." CatTime.com. <http://cattime.com/cat-
    breeds/persian-cats#/slide/1>

"Persian." VetStreet. <http://www.vetstreet.com/cats/
    persian#0_sb32r7w2>

"Persian Cat." Petfinder. <https://www.petfinder.com/cat-
    breeds/Persian>

"Ragdoll." The International Cat Association.
    <http://tica.org/nl/cat-breeds/item/254>

"Persian Breed Standard." CFA.org. <http://cfa.org/Portals/0/
    documents/breeds/standards/persian.pdf >

"Portosystemic Shunt." Cornell University College of
    Veterinary Medicine. <http://www.vet.cornell.edu/
    fhc/Health_Information/PortosystemicShunt.cfm>

"Progressive Retinal Atrophy/Degeneration in Cats (PRS,
    PRD)." PetEducation.com.

<http://www.peteducation.com/ article.cfm?c=1+2124&aid=342>

"Teacup Persian Health Problems." Teacup Cats and Kittens. <http://www.teacupcatsandkittens.com/teacup-persian-health/>

"The Hybrid Cat Breeds of the World." Cat Breed Info. <http://www.cat-breed-info.com/hybrid-cat-breeds.html>

"Urine Crystals and Bladder Stones in Cats: Formation, Diet and Other Treatment." PetEducation.com. <http://www.peteducation.com/article.cfm?c=1+2142&aid =2729>

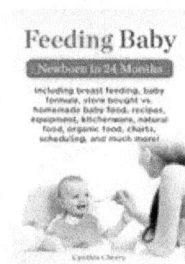

Feeding Baby
Cynthia Cherry
978-1941070000

Axolotl
Lolly Brown
978-0989658430

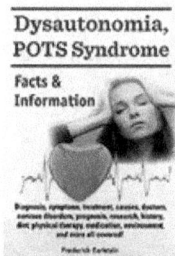

Dysautonomia, POTS
Syndrome
Frederick Earlstein
978-0989658485

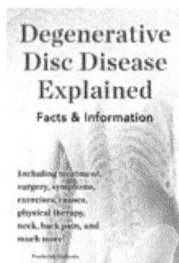

Degenerative Disc
Disease Explained
Frederick Earlstein
978-0989658485

Sinusitis, Hay Fever,
Allergic Rhinitis Explained
Frederick Earlstein
978-1941070024

Wicca
Riley Star
978-1941070130

Zombie Apocalypse
Rex Cutty
978-1941070154

Capybara
Lolly Brown
978-1941070062

Eels As Pets
Lolly Brown
978-1941070167

Scabies and Lice Explained
Frederick Earlstein
978-1941070017

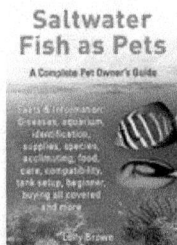

Saltwater Fish As Pets
Lolly Brown
978-0989658461

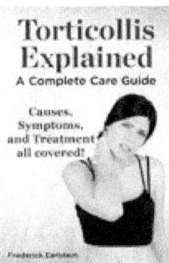

Torticollis Explained
Frederick Earlstein
978-1941070055

Kennel Cough
Lolly Brown
978-0989658409

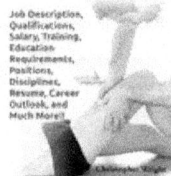

Physiotherapist, Physical
Therapist
Christopher Wright
978-0989658492

Rats, Mice, and Dormice
As Pets
Lolly Brown
978-1941070079

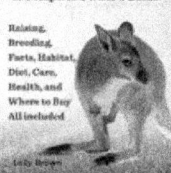

Wallaby and Wallaroo Care
Lolly Brown
978-1941070031

Bodybuilding Supplements
Explained
Jon Shelton
978-1941070239

Demonology
Riley Star
978-19401070314

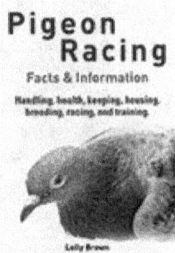

Pigeon Racing
Lolly Brown
978-1941070307

Dwarf Hamster
Lolly Brown
978-1941070390

Cryptozoology
Rex Cutty
978-1941070406

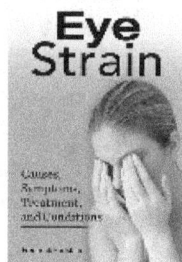

Eye Strain
Frederick Earlstein
978-1941070369

Inez The Miniature Elephant
Asher Ray
978-1941070353

Vampire Apocalypse
Rex Cutty
978-1941070321

www.ingramcontent.com/pod-product-compliance
Lightning Source LLC
LaVergne TN
LVHW051639080426
835511LV00016B/2390